My Confirmation Memories

CONCORDIA PUBLISHING HOUSE · SAINT LOUIS

My God, accept my heart this day
And make it always Thine
That I from Thee no more may stray,
No more from Thee decline.

Anoint me with Thy Spirit's grace
And seal me for Thine own
That I may see Thy glorious face
And worship at Thy throne.

My Confirmation

____

was confirmed in the Christian faith

at ____

on ____

____

Pastor

My confirmation verse

____

____

____

____

____

The Shepherd Psalm

The Lord is my shepherd, I shall not be in want.
He makes me lie down in green pastures,
He leads me beside quiet waters, He restores my soul.
He guides me in the paths of righteousness
for His name's sake.

Even though I walk through the valley
of the shadow of death,
I will fear no evil, for You are with me;
Your rod and Your staff, they comfort me.

You prepare a table before me
in the presence of my enemies.
You anoint my head with oil; my cup overflows.
Surely goodness and love will follow me
all the days of my life,
and I will dwell in the house of the Lord forever.

My Baptism

____

was baptized in the Christian faith

at ____

on ____

____

Godparent/sponsor

____

Godparent/sponsor

____

Pastor

You are no longer foreigners and aliens, but fellow citizens with God's people and members of God's household, built on the foundation of the apostles and prophets, with Christ Jesus Himself as the chief cornerstone. In Him the whole building is joined together and rises to become a holy temple in the Lord. And in Him you too are being built together to become a dwelling in which God lives by His Spirit.

Ephesians 2:19–22

My Confirmation Invitation

My Confirmation Certificate

The Lord's Prayer

Our Father who art in heaven,
Hallowed be Thy name.
Thy kingdom come.
Thy will be done on earth as it is in heaven.
Give us this day our daily bread.
And forgive us our trespasses,
as we forgive those who trespass against us.
And lead us not into temptation,
But deliver us from evil.
For Thine is the kingdom and the power and the glory
forever and ever. Amen.

Photographs of My Life until Now

My Confirmation Photograph

My Class Photograph

Gifts and Cards

My Favorite Bible Verses

Pictures of My Family and Friends

Pictures of My Family and Friends

The Lord's Supper

Our Lord Jesus Christ, in the night
in which He was betrayed,
took bread; and when He had given thanks,
He broke it and gave it to His disciples, saying,
"Take, eat; this is My body,
which is given for you.
This do in remembrance of Me."

After the same manner also He took the cup after supper,
and when He had given thanks,
He gave it to them, saying,
"Drink of it, all of you.
This cup is the New Testament in My blood,
which is shed for you and for many
for the remission of sins.
This do, as often as you drink it,
in remembrance of Me."

The Apostles' Creed

I believe in God, the Father Almighty
maker of heaven and earth.
And in Jesus Christ, His only Son, our Lord,
who was conceived by the Holy Spirit,
born of the virgin Mary,
suffered under Pontius Pilate,
was crucified, died and was buried.
He descended into hell.
The third day He rose again from the dead.
He ascended into heaven
and sits at the right hand of God the Father Almighty.
From thence He will come to judge the living and the dead.

I believe in the Holy Spirit,
the holy Christian Church,
the communion of saints,
the forgiveness of sins,
the resurrection of the body,
and the life everlasting. Amen.

Your Faithful Shepherd

I am the Good Shepherd.
The Good Shepherd gives His life for the sheep. . . .
I know My sheep as the Father knows Me.
My sheep know Me as I know the Father.
So I give My life for My sheep.
I also have other sheep
that are not from this pen.
I must lead them.
They, too, will respond to My voice,
So they will be one flock with one Shepherd.

God's Word ®

Let me be Thine forever,
Thou faithful God and Lord;
Let me forsake Thee never
Nor wander from Thy Word.
Lord, do not let me waver,
But give me steadfastness,
And for such grace forever
Thy holy name I'll bless.

He who began a good work in you will carry it on to completion until the day of Christ Jesus.

Be faithful, even to the point of death, and I will give you the crown of life.

Copyright © 1974, 1994 by Concordia Publishing House
3558 S. Jefferson Avenue, St. Louis, MO 63118-3968
1-800-325-3040 • cph.org

Manufactured in Dongguan, China/055760/416139

13 14 15 16 17 18 19 20 21 30 29 28 27 26 25 24 23 22